Operation Pastorius: The History of the Nazi Intelligence Operation to Commit Sabotage in the United States during World War II

By Charles River Editors

Admiral Wilhelm Canaris, chief of the *Abwehr* during the war

About Charles River Editors

Charles River Editors provides superior editing and original writing services across the digital publishing industry, with the expertise to create digital content for publishers across a vast range of subject matter. In addition to providing original digital content for third party publishers, we also republish civilization's greatest literary works, bringing them to new generations of readers via ebooks.

Sign up here to receive updates about free books as we publish them, and visit Our Kindle Author Page to browse today's free promotions and our most recently published Kindle titles.

Introduction

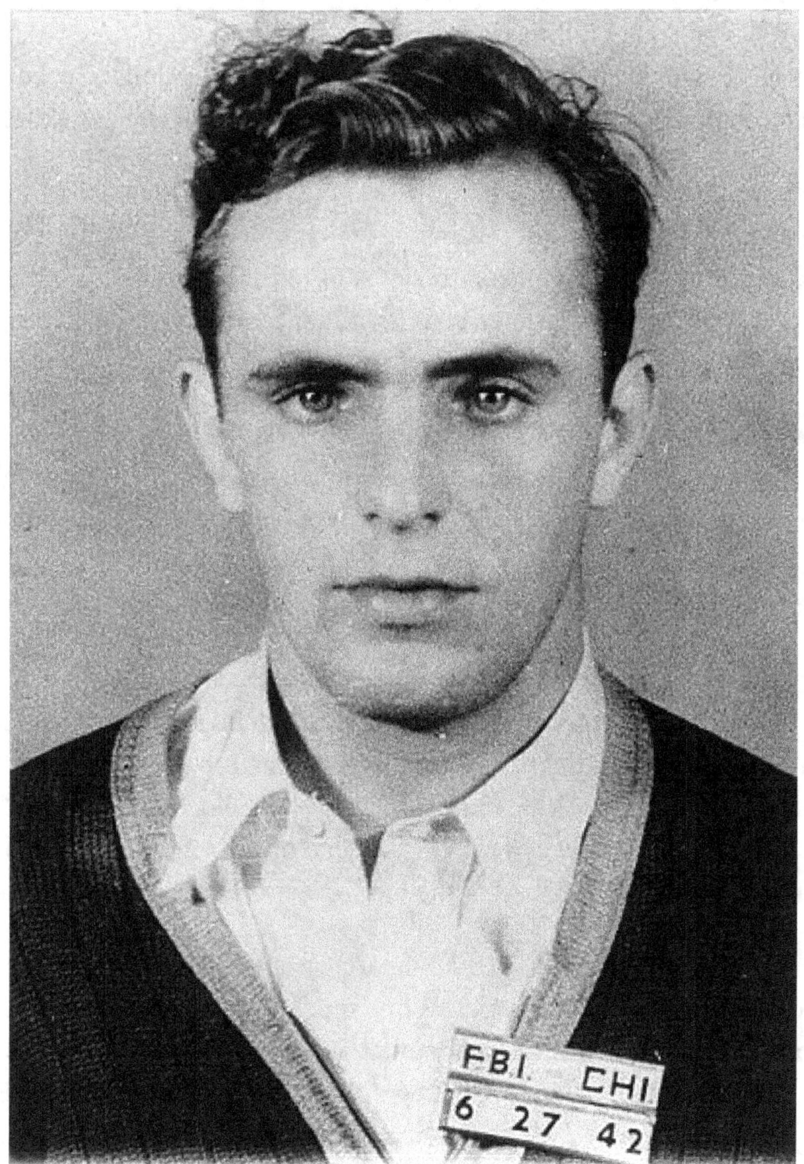

Herbert Haupt, one of the Nazi agents

"Hostile armies may face each other for years, striving for the victory which is decided in a single day. This being so, to remain in ignorance of the enemy's condition simply because one grudges the outlay of a hundred ounces of silver in honors and emoluments, is the height of inhumanity." – Sun Tzu on the utility of intelligence and spying, "Art of War," Chapter 13.

World War II stood apart in many ways from every earlier war, not least in the way that it reached to every corner of the planet and involved a noticeable segment of humanity's collective resources. Battles erupted not only on land and the sea's surface as they had for centuries, but also in the ocean depths and the windswept heights of the sky.

Nearly every conceivable terrain saw use as a battlefield: the neat farmland and small towns of Western Europe; the streets of major cities; storm-swept ocean at the edge of the Arctic Ice; tropical swamps and jungles; thick forests; open steppes stretching for hundreds of miles; sandy and stony deserts in North Africa; picturesque tropical islands and atolls; frozen tundra; the slopes of active volcanoes; rugged mountain ranges; and many other regions of the globe.

One of the war's most crucial struggles happened in the realm of the unseen, inside the human mind and amid the invisible flow of radio waves. Every war is a battle of wits as intelligence-gathering, tactics, and strategies clash, from the level of individual action up to the grand, overarching schemes of generals and statesmen. Intelligence took on a freshly urgent aspect in World War II, however, as the fate of offensives, armies, and nations came to hang on the struggle to decrypt vital enemy radio traffic and military communications.

During the Second World War, cryptography suddenly became a significant factor in warfare because of mid-20th century advances in communications technology. With radios small and common enough to be fitted into most individual vehicles and readily carried in a man-portable form, information and orders flowed from supreme headquarters to individual squad leaders, tanks, and soldiers at the front and back again.

Complex radio networks connected armies to their other elements almost like a nervous system, making unprecedented tactical and strategic coordination between units hundreds of miles apart not only possible but swift and, in some cases, efficient. Decrypting these signals or protecting their contents from enemy spying became one of the touchstones of victory or defeat. "Information warfare" arrived well ahead of the modern computer and satellite networks.

At a more personal level, the struggle to gain the upper hand in intelligence sometimes resembled the plot of a pulp adventure novel. While much of the hard work occurred in bland offices located in British manor houses, government buildings, or American labs, moments of intense human drama also punctuated the cryptographic struggle as soldiers, spies, and others risked their lives to gain a fresh key to crack a heretofore impenetrable code, or underwent similar risks attempting to keep the secret.

By the end of 1941, it seemed as if nothing could stop Germany. German forces had swept deep into Russia, killing or capturing hundreds of thousands of prisoners and were closing in on Moscow. In North Africa, German and Italian forces under the command of General Erwin Rommel were poised to take British-controlled Egypt. In the Atlantic, German U-boats were sinking such large numbers of British merchant ships that it seemed as if Britain might be starved into submission.

The Japanese attack on Pearl Harbor presented President Franklin D. Roosevelt with a strategic problem that went beyond how to deal with Japanese aggression. Although the war in Europe had been raging for more than two years, many Americans felt it was not their concern, especially with the ultimate defeat of the British seeming all but certain. Roosevelt had done as much as possible to aid Britain short of being drawn into the war, providing American ships, tanks, and other weapons, and once Pearl Harbor brought America into the war, he believed that Nazi Germany posed as much of a threat to the country as Japan.

Four days after the attack on Pearl Harbor, Hitler declared war on America, almost casually and without seeming to consider the consequences. There was no diplomatic necessity for him to have done this and no obvious strategic reason. Germany's military successes were so complete at that point that Hitler seemed to believe declaring war on one more country was a trifling matter.

In some ways, he was right, because in December 1941, the US Army was tiny and poorly equipped. In September 1939, the German army invading Poland comprised 100 infantry divisions and six panzer divisions. At that time, the whole US Army was comprised of just five divisions. Even two years later, the US Army was relatively small and ill-equipped. It was clear that, in strictly military terms, the United States was no threat to Nazi Germany when Hitler declared war in late 1941.

However, American industry had the capacity and power ahead of virtually any other country in the world, so if America posed a threat to Germany, it would be through its capacity to produce weapons, tanks, aircraft, and ships in vast numbers. At the same time, America was simply too far from any German-controlled airbases to make strategic bombing a possibility. Thus, if a direct attack on American industry was not feasible, the best alternative was to mount a campaign of subterfuge and sabotage.

The responsibility for mounting an attack on American industry was given to the German military secret intelligence service, the *Abwehr*, which devised a plan to land saboteurs in America to attack factories, railroads, and perhaps conduct a random bombing campaign against American civilians. The Nazi plan was given the codename of Operation Pastorius, and it was launched in June 1942, just six months after Germany had declared war on America. What followed was one of World War II's most bizarre spy stories.

Operation Pastorius: The History of the Nazi Intelligence Operation to Commit Sabotage in the United States during World War II looks at one of the war's most unique operations. Along with pictures of important people, places, and events, you will learn about the operation like never before.

The *Abwehr* at the Start of the War

America and Germany found themselves at war during World War One, which began in August 1914 when Germany, Austria-Hungary, and Italy fought against the Triple Entente of Britain, France, and Russia. The United States was not directly a part of this war, but its industrial capacity made it an important source of munitions and materials, especially for countries in the Triple Entente. Since America was neutral, it was free to sell goods to any country, but in practice, most of the trade was with France, Britain, and Russia.

This became a source of concern for Germany at an early stage, and America was finally drawn into the war in April 1917 after it was discovered that German agents were attempting to incite the Mexican government to declare war on the United States. But even before that point, Germany had attempted to find ways to reduce the supply of materials from America to France and Britain, and one of the people involved in this effort was Wilhelm Franz Canaris. Canaris was born in 1887 in Aplerbeck, Westphalia. His father, Carl, was a wealthy industrialist, but rather than pursuing a career in the family business, Canaris joined the Imperial German Navy in 1905 at the age of 18. Upon completing his training in 1911, he was assigned to serve on SMS *Dresden*, a light cruiser. *Dresden* spent time in the Mediterranean before being sent to the Caribbean to protect German settlers during the Mexican Revolution, and though the ship was due to return to Germany in 1914, the declaration of war in August of that year meant that the ship instead made its way to the Pacific Ocean to become a part of *Vizeadmiral* Maximilian von Spee's East Asia Squadron.

Canaris

By that time, Canaris, who had been promoted to lieutenant, was serving as the ship's intelligence officer, a role to which he was eminently suited. He was ferociously intelligent and fluent in six languages, and when the *Dresden* found itself the sole German survivor of the Battle of the Falkland Islands on December 8, 1914, Canaris played an important role in helping the ship hide from the Royal Navy while attacking British merchant shipping. The *Dresden* was able to evade detection for three months until, on March 14th, out of coal and low on ammunition, the ship was scuttled off the Chilean port of Más a Fuera.

The entire crew was interned, but it soon became clear that Canaris had no intention of spending the war in an internment camp. Shortly after arriving, Canaris escaped, having first sought the permission of his commanding officer. After a grueling eight month trip across the Andes, he arrived in Buenos Aires, and from there, he took a Dutch liner, the *Frisia*, to Plymouth. Most of the passengers aboard were English, but Canaris' language abilities were good enough to persuade them that he was a Chilean with an English mother. He used the voyage to study English habits and mannerisms, and when he arrived in Plymouth, he was allowed to take a ship to Rotterdam and make his way back to Germany from there.

Canaris' effective work as intelligence officer aboard the *Dresden* and his long and rather romantic journey from the Chilean internment camp back to Germany made him something of a minor hero within the Imperial German Navy; however, there was some doubt as to how his obvious skills and abilities might be put to use. In Germany, as in most other countries at the time, the notion of an intelligence service was new and abhorrent to many military officers. One senior German officer had specifically forbidden the establishment of such a service because it would expose his officers to "people of dubious reputation." When the Kaiser was finally persuaded to allow the establishment of an office of military intelligence, he did so with the understanding that it would comprise no more than a dozen officers.

The German military intelligence service, known only as Section IIIB, slowly grew under the leadership of Walther Nicolai, a Prussian officer of impeccable credentials who saw the importance of intelligence. Given that Canaris had shown himself capable of surviving in enemy territory and had been able to pass himself off as half-English, it was no surprise that he was recruited to join IIIB. Canaris was assigned a role in Madrid, Spain, where he successfully set up a network of agents involved in reporting the movement of allied shipping to German U-boats. This mission was so successful that Canaris was awarded the Iron Cross First Class when he returned to Germany in 1917, and he was also rewarded by being given command of his own U-Boat.

During the period when Canaris was with Section IIIB, German intelligence is thought to have pulled-off its most audacious mission in America. In Jersey City, opposite the Statue of Liberty, the one-mile-long Black Tom pier and associated warehouses and railroad lines were the main nexus for shipping cargo to Europe. Many of these involved consignments of weapons, munitions, and explosives. On the night of July 29th/30th 1916, it was believed that freight cars, warehouses, barges, and freighters at the Black Tom complex were carrying anything up to 4,000,000 pounds of explosives.

At around 02:00 a.m., flames suddenly erupted from at least one freight car and one barge. Around eight minutes later, the Black Tom complex was rocked by a series of mammoth explosions in which windows were broken up to twenty-five miles away from the blast, and residents in Philadelphia, ninety miles away, were woken by the explosion. Debris continued to fall from the sky for up to two hours after the first explosion. Perhaps the most surprising aspect of the explosion was the few casualties it caused—up to seven people are thought to have died in the blast though some sources suggest the true number may be only four.

The damage to the Black Tom complex was so severe that it was difficult for investigators to tell what had happened. It was initially believed that an accidental fire might have caused the explosion when it was discovered that workmen had lit smudge pots to keep mosquitoes away the previous evening, but this seemed unlikely. The only other option appeared to be deliberate sabotage. The blasts had destroyed a huge stockpile of munitions and explosives destined for the Russian and Western Front, the value of cargo and property destroyed estimated at $20,000,000 (around $500,000,000 present-day value). Was it possible that an agent or agents had deliberately caused the explosion to prevent these materials from reaching the allied armies?

The body assigned the task of investigation was the Bureau of Investigation—the precursor to the FBI—created in 1909. However, the bureau had less than 250 fifty employees across America, and it had little experience investigating these types of crime. Irish and Chinese nationals were questioned, though naturally, suspicion fell more strongly upon Germany.

The investigation revealed a number of suspects, including the charming and popular German ambassador to the United States, Johann Heinrich von Bernstorff, but no arrests were made, and no charges brought. The sabotage of American industry continued with several other explosions and the loss of a number of cargo ships, believed to have been the result of bombs in their holds.

It is now known that the Black Tom explosion and other acts of industrial sabotage were caused by German agents operating in America, partly organized by von Bernstorff. This was not formally recognized until 1939 when a German-American Mixed Claims Commission found the German government responsible for the explosion.

What remains unclear is the involvement of Section IIIB or whether Wilhelm Canaris was directly involved in planning these acts of terrorism in America. He was certainly working for Section IIIB at the time, and at the very least, he must have been aware of German agents operating in America and the acts of sabotage they carried out. By the time Germany had once more found itself war with America in 1941, the need to limit the production of American industry was just as great as it had been during the First World War. By that time, Canaris was one of the most important figures in German military intelligence.

The military defeat of Germany, culminating in the Armistice of November 1918, brought peace to Europe, but it also brought a period of convulsive change for Germany. The Kaiser was forced to abdicate, and Imperial Germany—re-named the Weimar Republic—was ruled by its first elected government. However, the early years of democratic rule were anything but stable.

The Communist revolution in Russia inspired many disaffected soldiers and sailors in Germany. In the period immediately following the Armistice, several groups seized control of areas of Germany, and "Free Socialist Republics" were declared. For three months, from November 1918-January 1919, the German government was re-named the "Council of the People's Deputies," and it seemed possible that Germany, like Russia, might become a Communist state.

The remnants of the German Army—reduced to only 100,000 men by the terms of the Armistice—and several Freikorps—essentially private armies composed of soldiers returning from the front—crushed what later became known as the November Revolution. The leaders of the revolutionary movement were quietly murdered, and a shaky calm returned to Germany.

However, the brief surge toward Communism terrified senior members of the German military, and many became life-long anti-Communists as a direct result.

One of these was Wilhelm Canaris. After surrendering his U-boat, Canaris returned to the Admiralty in Berlin, where he was appointed as a liaison officer with the Guards' Cavalry. Soon after, he was posted to the Navy base at Kiel. Ostensibly, his role was to take responsibility for training young officers, but from the start, Canaris was involved in clandestine operations.

The Treaty of Versailles ending World War One contained a number of clauses intended to prevent Germany from amassing a large army or navy. In particular, there were strict limits on the number of men who could serve in each, and for the navy, on the number and types of ships they were permitted to operate. The treaty limited the German Navy to a total of no more than 15,000 men, of whom only 1,500 were to be officers. While seeming to abide by this, Canaris was busy building up a secret reserve of navy officers who could be called up at short notice if required. In 1924, he was sent on a secret mission to Japan to organize the building of U-Boats for the German Navy in Japanese shipyards. He also negotiated a number of secret agreements with the Spanish government. Although his role was still officially that of the head of navy training, Canaris was building a reputation as a man who had a particular aptitude for secret work. Then, in December 1932, Canaris was appointed captain of the training cruiser, *Schlesien*. It seemed that his secret work was probably finished, but only two months later, Germany elected a new chancellor: Adolf Hitler.

Like many Germans, Canaris and many other naval officers were skeptical about the upstart Austrian and his grandiose ideas, but like many Germans, most naval officers saw Hitler's appointment as a barrier to the further spread of communism in Germany. When it became clear that the new chancellor intended to ignore the Treaty of Versailles and increase the size and power of the navy, many naval officers became supporters of Hitler and the Nazis.

By this time, Canaris' career had hit a major barrier. His relationship with his commanding officer, the arrogant and pompous Rear Admiral Max Bastian, had been deteriorating for some time. Bastian had claimed that Canaris had not treated him with due deference, and Canaris found the bumptious Bastien unbearable. In September 1934, this deteriorating relationship led to Canaris receiving an appointment that amounted to a punishment: he was made commander of naval defenses at Swinemunde. This, in effect, put him in charge of many miles of desolate, windswept beaches on East Prussia's Baltic coast. For someone who had been involved in the very heart of the German attempt to rebuild the navy, this posting must have been a bitter disappointment. Canaris spent much of his time riding the beaches and dunes of the rugged coast.

To most people, it seemed as if Canaris' career was all but over, but even as he served his time in exile, events were set in motion to bring him back to the center of intrigue and secret operations.

Although the Treaty of Versailles specifically forbade Germany from undertaking intelligence or espionage work, a new department, *Abwehr* (meaning "defense") was created within the Ministry of Defense. Initially, the purpose of *Abwehr* was to prevent espionage and spying in Germany, but within four years, the department had expanded into three distinct sections:

- Reconnaissance (which included the placement of German spies in other countries),

- Cipher and Radio Monitoring

- Counterespionage.

In its early days, *Abwehr* was a part of the German Army, but in 1929, General Kurt von Schleicher, an ambitious officer who had plans to make himself chancellor, combined *Abwehr* with the German naval intelligence unit to create a single intelligence agency for all branches of the German military.

Schleicher

Although its staff was mainly army officers, in 1932, a German naval officer, Captain Conrad Patzig, was appointed the leader of *Abwehr*. It was the first time a *Reichsmarine* officer was given control of a security organization, and in the topsy-turvy world of Nazi Germany, Patzig quickly discovered that his main rivals were not the intelligence organizations of other nations but other parts of the Nazi hierarchy. The *Schutzstaffel* (SS) began as personal bodyguards for Hitler, but when the Nazis came to power in Germany, it became more and more powerful. Under the leadership of Heinrich Himmler, the SS developed into a powerful paramilitary organization existing completely outside the control of the German government, owing allegiance only personally to Hitler. By 1934, the SS included two departments, which would become notorious: the *Geheime Staatspolizei,* which quickly became known as the Gestapo, and the *Sicherheitsdienst,* or SD, the security and intelligence service. The purpose of the Gestapo was to act as a secret police force, ensuring that any potential opposition to Nazi rule inside of

Germany would be crushed. The SD was approximately equivalent to *Abwehr*, responsible for gathering information on potential enemy nations and for conducting espionage activities outside of Germany.

While Himmler maintained control of the SS as a whole, he passed direct control of both the Gestapo and the SD to one of his most ruthless and able subordinates, Reinhard Heydrich. Heydrich, an ex-naval officer, shared Himmler's ambition to extend the power of the SS, and both men saw *Abwehr* as a direct rival of the SD. If possible, they wanted to have the military intelligence agency replaced by an organization completely controlled by the Nazis.

Himmler

Heydrich

Patzig

In late June 1934, the SS' growing power was dramatically demonstrated in what has become known as "The Night of the Long Knives." During an action to curb the power of another offshoot of the Nazi Party, the *Sturmabteilung* (SA), many members of the organization were arbitrarily executed by the SS. Himmler and Heydrich, with Hitler's agreement, also took the opportunity to remove a number of actual or potential rivals for power. General Kurt von Schleicher, the man who had created the new *Abwehr*, was murdered in his home by SS killers. Schleicher had committed no crime, but he was seen by the leaders of the Nazi movement as a potential rival, so he was killed to neutralize this possible threat. It was becoming clear that opposition to the Nazis or to the SS was a very risky business.

Within this atmosphere of terror and repression, Captain Patzig, head of *Abwehr*, found himself in a difficult and dangerous position. There was no doubt that the leaders of the SS wanted *Abwehr* disbanded and its responsibilities taken over by the SS, but the SS was not yet powerful enough to directly challenge the German Army itself. Instead, it undermined *Abwehr*'s activities and criticized them to Hitler.

Eventually, things came to a head in late 1934 over the issue of clandestine overflights of Polish territory. These had been ordered by Patzig to obtain photographs of border defense, but

Hitler had signed a non-aggression pact with Poland in early 1934, and he was concerned these flights would put the pact at risk, so Patzig was ordered to cease the flights. He refused, and in early 1935, he was fired as head of *Abwehr*. The SS would have preferred to have *Abwehr* replaced entirely by the SD, but it was not yet ready to do so. As a result, the search began for a replacement head of the intelligence service acceptable to both the German military, the SS, and the Nazis.

Heydrich, by now the head of the SD and Gestapo, had started his military career in the German Navy in 1922. His ambition and ability led to rapid promotion, and by 1928, he was *Oberleutnant zur See*. In 1930, he met Lina von Osten, daughter of a minor German aristocrat, and the two soon announced they were engaged to be married. It was, however, said that Heydrich was already engaged to another woman, and in early 1931, he was dismissed from the navy for "conduct unbecoming an officer and a gentleman." Within nine months of leaving the navy, Heydrich had married Lina and joined both the Nazi Party and the SS, but he never forgot that during the period when the navy had investigated his conduct, one of his former commanding officers spoke up on his behalf: Wilhelm Canaris. Heydrich believed Canaris was someone with whom he could work, so in January 1935, Canaris was abruptly recalled from exile in Swinemunde and appointed as the new head of *Abwehr*.

Recognizing that the rivalry with the Gestapo and SD was one of the main issues for *Abwehr*, Canaris spent a great deal of time working directly with Heydrich to establish clear responsibilities for each service. This led to the signing of an agreement between Heydrich and Canaris in the mid-1930s that set out precisely what each organization would be responsible for in relation to the other, but even as the two men worked together extensively, it was clear that they remained suspicious of each other. Privately, Canaris referred to Heydrich as a "brutal fanatic." Heydrich was equally concerned about Canaris, respecting his obvious intelligence but deeply distrustful of his loyalty to the Nazis. Canaris (rightly) suspected Heydrich of using SD operatives to spy on *Abwehr* and intercept telephone calls and documents. In 1935, Canaris was promoted to the rank of rear admiral. *Abwehr* seemed to have settled its differences with the SS, and within two years of his taking charge, *Abwehr* expanded from a staff of 150 people to more than 1,000.

There seemed little doubt at the time that Canaris was an enthusiastic supporter of Hitler and the Nazis. Deeply anti-Semitic, it was Canaris who had first suggested that Jews in Germany be forced to identify themselves by wearing the Star of David, something that would later become associated with brutal persecution and ultimately genocide.

Furthermore, under Canaris' leadership, *Abwehr* conducted a number of successful intelligence operations against other European countries. For example, when the Spanish Civil War began in 1936, Germany, like many other European countries, signed an agreement prohibiting the supply of weapons or munitions to either side. However, by using his international connections, Canaris

was able to ensure that General Franco's Nationalists were supplied with both, and when
Germany occupied Austria in 1938, Canaris was one of the first senior officers to arrive in
Vienna, seizing documents relating to Austrian military intelligence operations and eventually
absorbing virtually the whole Austrian intelligence service into *Abwehr*.

In many ways, Canaris seemed an unlikely spymaster. At just under 5'4, he was only barely
tall enough to join the navy, and while he was intelligent, he was soft-spoken and regarded by
most people who met him as a "gentleman." In fact, his role as head of *Abwehr* was generally not
known outside of a small circle of senior military and SS personnel. The British intelligence
services, for example, were confident that the head of *Abwehr* was a senior German Army
officer, General Kurt von Tippelskirch, who was actually the quartermaster general of the
Wehrmacht. When a spy scandal involving a senior Polish officer (a scandal partly engineered
by Canaris) erupted in 1938 and Canaris visited Count Lipski, the Polish Ambassador to
Germany, Lipski later wrote, "I was visited by an elderly white-haired Admiral. I was struck by
his soft benevolent manner and I never dreamed this was the chief of German intelligence."[1]

While he remained mysterious to the outside world, Canaris' careful, systematic approach to
intelligence gathering and espionage gradually gained him respect within the German military.
At the same time, however, Canaris was becoming disenchanted with Hitler and the Nazis. At
first, this was entirely pragmatic, because after the occupation of Czechoslovakia, it was clear to
most people that Poland would be Hitler's next target. Poland had alliances in place alliances
with both France and Britain, so if Germany went to war with Poland, it seemed likely it would
also find itself at war with Britain and France. Canaris had no moral objection to war - he simply
felt that Germany was not militarily strong enough to fight both Britain and France, and he was
horrified that Hitler seemed willing to take such a risk.

On September 1, 1939, German forces invaded Poland, and two days later, Britain and France
declared war on Germany. World War II had indeed begun, but Canaris' fears and those of other
German military officers appeared unfounded when Poland was defeated in just over a month.
After a period of relative quiet during the winter of 1939-1940, Germany invaded Norway and
Denmark in April 1940, and in May, German troops invaded Belgium, Holland, and
Luxembourg. The German invasions were stunning successes - by the end of June, France had
surrendered, and Norway, Denmark, Holland, Belgium, and Luxembourg had been occupied.
Hitler, it seemed, had been right to believe that Germany was strong enough to challenge the best
armies in Europe, and the country's rapid victories suggested the Nazis were unstoppable.

In late 1940, only Britain remained at war with Germany, but the Royal Air Force's ability to
fight off the Luftwaffe meant that Hitler's plan to invade Britain across the English Channel was
abandoned. Hitler did not seem overly concerned at the time, because in military terms, Britain
simply was not in a position to directly confront Germany. Moreover, he had already turned his

---

[1] Colvin 1951

attention to the country that had always been the target of his most dramatic plans: the Soviet Union.

Germany had signed a non-aggression pact with the Soviet Union just before launching the attack on Poland, but this was never anything more than a ploy to prevent Soviet troops from coming to Poland's aid. Hitler's intention had always been to attack Russia, both to neutralize the threat of communism and to seize the land he believed Germany needed.

With Canaris and other dubious German officers having been proved emphatically wrong about Hitler's leadership and Nazi Germany's military capabilities (at least thus far), few opposed Hitler's plans to invade Russia. Communism was still seen by the majority of high-ranking German officers as a threat not just to Germany, but to the world order, and at this time only a select few doubted that a German invasion of Russia would succeed just as quickly and dramatically as the invasions of Western European countries. As such, when the Wehrmacht crossed the Russian frontier in June 1941, there was little opposition from most Germans.

For Canaris, however, the situation was different. As head of *Abwehr*, he had traveled to Poland in the wake of the German invasion, and he had seen the massacres that followed and was sickened by them. Following a meeting with General Wilhelm Keitel, head of *Oberkommando der Wehrmacht* (German Military High Command), he wrote, "I told Keitel I was aware of extensive executions planned in Poland and that the nobility and clergy particularly were to be exterminated. The *Wehrmacht* would in the final reckoning be held responsible for these atrocities carried out under their very noses."

Keitel

Keitel was unmoved, telling Canaris the executions were being carried out on direct orders from Hitler and that nothing could be done to change them. When he became aware of the intention to invade Russia, Canaris understood it would lead to far more atrocities. Almost alone amongst the most senior German officers, he objected to what Hitler was doing on moral as well as practical grounds.

The invasion of Russia initially went precisely as Hitler had anticipated, with German forces making massive territorial gains and taking vast numbers of Russian prisoners. However, the Soviets did not surrender, and by the end of 1941, the Germans found themselves facing not just increasing resistance but also a bitter winter. For the first time, the seemingly unstoppable German advance faltered and then stopped, and mud, snow, and dogged opposition made further progress impossible.

It was at this point that the Japanese Navy attacked the American fleet at Pearl Harbor. Almost as an afterthought, possibly because he was distracted by a lack of progress in Russia, Hitler also declared war on America. Given that the German military was almost completely committed to the invasion of Russia, there was little to be done to attack the United States directly. Instead, Hitler would turn to *Abwehr* to find ways to undermine American industrial power.

The *Abwehr* in America

Although a project like Operation Pastorius sounds daunting, the infiltration of *Abwehr* agents into America actually began long before the declaration of war in December 1941. In fact, when Canaris inherited command of *Abwehr* in 1935, he found an existing network of agents already in place in the United States, and he immediately began to expand this group.

Canaris undertook a major reorganization of *Abwehr* in 1938, as the organization had become so large it was difficult to control. There was, however, another reason for the change in structure. In 1937, the headquarters of *Abwehr* at 76/78 Tirpitzufer in Berlin, close to the building housing the military high command, was the subject of a number of burglaries. In several cases, documents were stolen both from headquarters and field stations, and fires were started to conceal what had been removed. The perpetrators were none other than special teams sent by the SS.

Meanwhile, Soviet leader Joseph Stalin began a series of purges against members of his military. Up to 35,000 high-ranking officers were killed or imprisoned during a two-year period, often on trumped up charges. Stalin had become afraid of the Red Army's growing power, and the purges were to ensure that only senior officers who were absolutely loyal to him remained. Hitler became aware of this and understood that some of the most experienced and able officers in the Soviet Army were being eliminated. Knowing that he intended war with the Soviet Union at some point in the future, this suited Hitler perfectly as the loss of these officers made the Russians considerably less effective as a fighting force.

There was, at the time, regular contact between German and Russian officers, and Germany was still using Russian facilities for training and the testing and evaluation of new weapons. As a result, Hitler was concerned that German officers might become aware of the purges and try to warn their Russian counterparts. In any rational state, the logical response would have been a prohibition on the sharing of such information, but that was not how things worked in Nazi Germany; instead, Himmler and Heydrich persuaded Hitler that the best way forward was to burgle the *Abwehr* offices and steal any information they had relating to the purges. Members of the Gestapo's criminal division were recruited to carry out the burglaries.

It seems likely that Canaris was aware of the identity of the burglars because little attempt was made to trace them, but *Abwehr* was reorganized to bring it more tightly under Canaris' control. The organization was divided into three main departments - Section I was responsible for espionage abroad, Section II was responsible for the sabotage of enemy (and potential enemy) military and industrial strength, and Section III was responsible for counter-espionage within Germany.

Canaris often carried out the recruitment of agents for Sections I and II. If he had a failing as a leader, it was his inability to delegate, and he liked to personally vet prospective new members of the organization. The people recruited were often disaffected foreign nationals, and few had any experience when it came to spying. This was not such a problem for F-Agents (*Friedensagent*) who were sent abroad in peacetime to gather scientific, technical, political, economic, and military information. However, for A-Agents (*Kriegsagenten*), those sent into enemy countries during wartime, the lack of training was a major problem.

America was a prime destination for F-Agents in the years before the war, when a number of organizations sympathetic to the Nazis emerged in America. For example, members of the German-American Bund wore a Nazi-style uniform complete with swastika emblems, and other groups, such as the Silver Shirts and the Ku Klux Klan, approved of Hitler's anti-Semitic racial theories. These organizations provided fertile ground for the recruitment of agents working for *Abwehr*.

Although *Abwehr* recruited many spies and followers in America, the operations they carried out were extremely amateurish. For example, in the late 1930s, Guenther Gustav Rumrich, an American citizen who had been born in Germany and had managed to fail at everything he attempted, wrote to Colonel Walter Nicolai, the man who had led German intelligence services during World War I. After reading Nicolai's memoirs, Rumrich to spy for Germany.

Nicolai passed the letter to *Abwehr*, and for about 20 months, Rumrich established a network of agents and Nazi sympathizers across America. He sent a great deal of information back to Germany, though little was of direct value, and the means by which this information was sent led to the discovery of the group. Rumrich wrote long letters to his immediate superior, Dr. Erich Pfeiffer of the Hamburg branch of the *Abwehr*, but rather than being sent directly, these were first mailed to a beauty parlor in Dundee, Scotland, after which they were re-routed to Hamburg. *Abwehr* seemed to believe that this would keep the stream of letters secret, but seeing so much mail coming from America, a postman in Dundee became suspicious and reported the matter to his superiors, who informed British intelligence. Since the letters carried a US postmark, the British informed the FBI, which eventually intercepted the letters and learned of Rumrich and his network through them.

When Rumrich was arrested in February 1938, not only did he immediately provide a full confession about his spy ring, but he also agreed to turn state's evidence and provide as much as he knew about *Abwehr* operations in America. The trial that followed in October 1938 shocked many Americans, who had no idea that Germany was spying there, and it actually led to a general hardening of attitudes toward Germany. However, to those who already knew about such things, the trial demonstrated that Rumrich's spy ring was bungling, ineffective, and conducted in a very amateurish way. That made it all the more concerning that this group had escaped the FBI's attention for almost two years. Although J. Edgar Hoover boasted after the trial that his agents had "smashed" a Nazi spy ring, the truth was that if it had not been for the curiosity of a Dundee postman, the FBI would have been completely unaware of the group's operations.

Despite this setback, *Abwehr* agents continued to operate in America, and at least two separate spy rings continued to send information back to Germany in the period between the declaration of war in Europe and the attack on Pearl Harbor. Canaris claimed he was operating a large and sophisticated network of agents within the United States, but German diplomats in America complained that these so-called agents were bungling idiots whose indiscretions were likely to antagonize American public opinion. For example, early in 1940, two men—Hausberger and Bergmann—turned-up at the German Embassy in Washington DC, where they explained to the astonished staff that they were freelance agents working for *Abwehr* and that they had been assigned a sabotage mission (they showed explosives to confirm this), but they had run out of cash. They asked the embassy for money so that they could continue with their mission, and during the angry exchange between German diplomats in America and *Abwehr* that followed, it was pointed out that such sabotage missions would endanger the already fragile relationship between the United States and Germany. It was also noted that the agents appeared to be completely witless, freely admitting freely to low-level embassy staff that they were German spies engaged in a sabotage mission. Initially, *Abwehr* denied knowing anything about Hausberger and Bergmann, and it was only under extreme pressure that Canaris admitted the two men might have been recruited as "observers." 10 days later, another *Abwehr* agent arrived at the embassy in Washington, asking for advice and help in setting up a short-wave radio.

Other *Abwehr* operations in America were just as compromised. The most successful spy ring was run by William G. Sebold, an American citizen who had visited Germany in 1939. He was arrested by the Gestapo, who threatened his German family unless he agreed to act as a German agent in America. Sebold agreed and was handed over to *Abwehr* Section I. Sebold proved to be the most successful German agent in America, recruiting a network of agents and using a radio to provide constant updates, but what *Abwehr* did not know was that Sebold was a double agent. After being approached by the Gestapo, he went straight to the American embassy in Berlin and told them what had happened. They suggested that it might be useful if he pretended to go along with what he was being asked to do, but from the time he returned to America, he was working for the FBI directly.

In March 1941, a man stepped off the sidewalk in Times Square in New York City, seemingly having looked the wrong way for oncoming traffic. He was struck and instantly killed by a taxi. Papers identified him as Julio Lopez Lido, but the FBI became suspicious, and an investigation revealed that the dead man was Ulrich von der Osten, an *Abwehr* agent sent to America to coordinate the actions of various spy rings.

In June 1941, the FBI arrested 33 men and women accused of being Nazi spies, and the information leading to these arrests came from Sebold. At the trial that followed, all the accused were found guilty and sentenced to long periods in prison.

Operation Pastorius

Up until December 1941, the efforts of *Abwehr* in America were bungling and inefficient, and most operations survived only because the FBI seemed equally inept. But naturally, when Germany declared war on America in December 1941, hunting for Nazi spies became much more serious, and this did not bode well when *Abwehr* was given a mission in 1942 to infiltrate agents into America to begin a campaign of sabotage.

Perhaps nothing illustrates the sheer naïveté of German intelligence operations better than the codename given to the operation that would attempt to infiltrate saboteurs into the United States. It is a basic precept of clandestine operations that an operational codename should not give any clue as to the nature of the operation, and to ensure this, British and American intelligence agencies used the random assignation of operational codenames. This led to some rather odd operational names, but it ensured that nothing would be deduced if the enemy became aware of the name.

However, the same concept did not seem to occur to the Germans responsible for naming secret operations. For example, in 1937, British agents became aware of a secret German project named Freya. Freya was a Norse goddess who, among other abilities, was able to see vast distances, even in the fog and rain. It did not require a great deal of mental effort to guess (correctly) that this was a project to develop an early-warning radar.

Given this history, it should not be a complete surprise to learn that when *Abwehr* was tasked with creating an operation to send agents to conduct sabotage in America in 1942, they named it "Operation Pastorius." In the late 1600s, Francis Daniel Pastorius founded Germantown, the first permanent German settlement in North America in what is now Pennsylvania. Pastorius was (and is) well-known both in America and Germany, and choosing this name for the operation would have made the intended target clear to everyone.

A bas relief depicting Pastorius

When Hitler demanded action against American industry in the spring of 1942, the arrests and trials of 1941 meant that *Abwehr* had few agents left in place in America. Canaris met with General Erwin von Lahousen, head of *Abwehr* Section II, to discuss Hitler's request, and the two men agreed that the only way to mount an effective operation would be to recruit new agents who could be landed on the East Coast. Lieutenant Walter Kappe, an officer working in Section II who had spent time living in America, was given the task of finding men suitable for the mission.

Lahousen

He used, as a starting point, the files of the *Deutsches Ausland-Institut,* an organization formed in 1917 to create favorable propaganda for Germany. After the end of World War I, it changed its function to focus on helping Germans wishing to emigrate, and it also maintained detailed files of German citizens who had spent time living abroad before returning to Germany. This was important because saboteurs chosen for Operation Pastorius would not only need to speak English, but also be familiar with American idioms and customs, which meant they would have ideally spent time living in America.

Kappe selected 12 potential members for the team, all currently serving in the German military or working in industrial plants associated with the production of military items. All 12 were offered incentives - if they agreed to take part in the mission, they would be exempt from future military service, and when they returned to Germany, they would be given well-paid jobs in safe areas. The 12 were sent to the *Abwehr* operational training camp located deep within a dense forest at Quentz Lake near the city of Brandenburg, west of Berlin. There, they were only permitted to converse in English while they were trained in the use of explosives and incendiary devices. They were taken on tours of German munitions factories and instructed about the most vulnerable pieces of equipment that could be most easily destroyed.

They were also instructed about their fictitious biographies. Each of the men had lived in America before returning to Germany, so this was relatively easy. All that was needed was a convincing cover story and documents to prove they had never left the United States. Each man was provided with forged documents that seemed to confirm that they had lived in America from the time they had first arrived there.

The urgency of the mission meant that the training period was severely curtailed. The 12 men were given just three weeks of training in all aspects of their mission. Given that none had any previous experience doing intelligence work, it could never have truly been expected to be enough, but nonetheless, at the end of the training period, nine of the 12 were selected to take part in Operation Pastorius. These nine men were divided into two separate groups, each of which was assigned a leader.

The oldest member of the group, 39-year-old George Dasch, was appointed leader of the first group. Dasch had lived in the United States from 1922-1941 and had spent time as a member of the US Army Air Corps. The group led by Dasch was comprised of four other men. Ernest Peter Burger had been an early Nazi follower and had taken part in the failed Beer Hall Putsch in the 1920s. He moved to America in 1927 and became a US citizen and member of the National Guard before returning to Germany in 1933 when Hitler became chancellor. Heinrich Heinck and Richard Quirin both moved to the US in 1927 and returned to Germany in 1939 when the Nazis offered to pay the travel expenses of any German willing to return home. The fifth member of the group was Joseph Schmidt, who had lived in Canada after emigrating there in the 1920s, but Schmidt had contracted gonorrhea while on leave from the training camp and was removed from the group, leaving Dasch's group with a total of four men.

Dasch

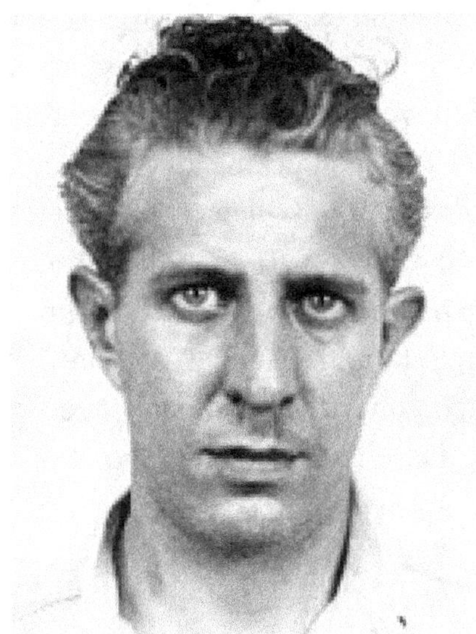

Quirin

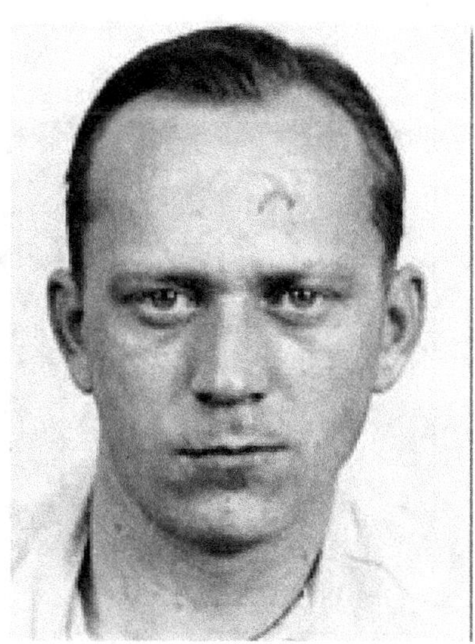

Heinck

The second group was led by Edward Kerling, another early enthusiast of the Nazi Party who had emigrated to America in the early 1930s. He returned to Germany in the summer of 1940, where he found work in the Nazi Propaganda Ministry in Berlin. Kerling's group was comprised of three men. Hermann Neubauer and Werner Thiel had emigrated to America in the 1930s before returning to Germany in 1940. The youngest member of the group, Herbert Hans Haupt, had moved to America in 1924 at the age of five and left to return to Germany in 1941, primarily to avoid the consequences of getting his girlfriend pregnant.

Thiel

Neubauer

These eight men, barely trained in the rudiments of sabotage and secret operations, were the entire force tasked with undertaking Operation Pastorius, a mission designated to sabotage as much American industry as possible. The plan for the group led by George Dasch was to be dropped by U-boat off of Long Island, New York, while Kerling's group was to be dropped off the coast of Florida.

Both groups were provided with waterproof crates of explosives, detonators, and incendiary devices. Many of the explosives were disguised as lumps of coal so they could be placed in the coal-stores of cargo ships and set to detonate when the ship was at sea. Both group leaders were told not to attempt to contact *Abwehr* by radio, but both were given white handkerchiefs on which the names and addresses of people sympathetic to the Nazi cause in America were written in invisible ink. They theoretically could be approached for assistance in an emergency.

In general, the choices of targets for sabotage were left up to the group leaders, but certain sites were highlighted as being of special importance. Aluminum production was assessed as being vital to the American war production, so aluminum plants in Tennessee, New York, and Illinois were identified as particularly important targets. The saboteurs were also expected to destroy railway lines and undertake a campaign of bombing random targets to undermine American civilian morale. Each team leader was also provided with $50,000 in cash with which to purchase weapons and additional explosives as required.

On May 26, 1942, Kerling and his group of three men left the French port of Lorient on U-584, bound for the coast of Florida. Two days later, Dasch and his group left the same harbor on U-202 bound for Long Island. Canaris and the leaders of *Abwehr* Section II settled back to wait for reports of death, destruction, and mayhem in America.

In the early hours of June 13, 1942, Dasch, his team, and their equipment and supplies were ferried on a small rubber boat from the U-boat to a lonely beach (now known as Atlantic Avenue Beach) on the shore of Long Island, not far from the town of Amagansett. All four wore German naval uniforms, with the hope that if they were captured upon landing, they could claim to be naval personnel rather than spies. The darkness and a light fog allowed them to land unobserved, so the four of them changed into civilian clothes.

They remained undetected for all of 30 minutes. By the summer of 1942, there was a night-curfew in effect for all Long Island beaches and regular patrols were carried out by Coast Guard personnel from a USCG station around half a mile from the beach. While Dasch and his team were still organizing themselves on the beach, 21-year-old John Cullen, an unarmed USCG seaman, ambled out of the fog as he patrolled the dunes near Amagansett, spotted the four men on the beach, and approached them.

Dasch took charge of the conversation that followed, and he could not have made himself and his team look any more suspicious. He claimed the four men had been on a fishing trip, though no boat was visible and the men were plainly not dressed for fishing. Cullen asked them to accompany him to the station, to which Dasch refused and blurted out, "Look, I wouldn't want to kill you. You don't know what this is all about." He then pulled a wad of bills from his pocket, gave it to Cullen, and told the young man to keep quiet about what he had seen.

While Dasch was speaking, Cullen heard other members of the group talking in a foreign language. Realizing that he was outnumbered and assuming the men were armed, Cullen accepted the bribe and walked casually off the beach, but as soon as he was out of the men's sight, he sprinted to the coast guard station and burst through the door, shouting, "There are Germans on the beach!"

Cullen and his coast guard colleagues returned to the beach, but there was no sign of the men. They did find a discarded pack of German cigarettes, and when it was lighter out, they discovered footprints leading to an area that had recently been covered up. An investigation revealed a large amount of buried cash as well as German naval uniforms, fuses, timers, and dynamite. A search ensued, but Dasch and his team had already caught a Long Island Railroad train to New York City.

Meanwhile, the USCG informed the FBI that a group of Germans seemed to have come ashore on the beach near Amagansett. FBI agents descended on Long Island and began to question local people, especially those believed to be Nazi sympathizers. This led nowhere other than an acceptance that the men had most likely taken a train to New York City, where the chances of finding them seemed very slim indeed.

Dasch and his team checked into a hotel in Manhattan later on June 13, and though the plan called for the four men to travel to Chicago, Dasch seemed to be in no hurry to begin the mission. The following day, Dasch called Ernest Burger into the hotel room while Quirin and Heinck were absent and told Burger that he hated Nazism and that he never had any intention of going through with the mission. Furthermore, he explained that he intended to give details of Operation Pastorius and its personnel to the FBI. He told Burger that he had a simple choice: help Dasch and the FBI or face almost certain arrest and execution as a spy. Burger readily agreed and said that he, too, would be happy to help the FBI and betray the other members of the group.

Later that day, on June 14, Dasch phoned the FBI's New York City office, but he was infuriated when the agent to whom he spoke refused to believe who he was. Dasch identified himself as "Franz Daniel Pastorius" and claimed that he had vital information from Germany that he would only give to J. Edgar Hoover in person. The agent most likely assumed it to be another prank call provoked by newspaper and radio reports of the apparent landing of four Germans on Long Island.

On June 17, a group of saboteurs led by Edward Kerling landed undetected on Ponte Vedra Beach, south of the city of Jacksonville, Florida. After having buried explosives on the beach, all four made their way to Jacksonville, where they caught a train bound for Cincinnati. After that, they split up, with two of them traveling by train to Chicago while the other two headed for New York City.

On the afternoon of Thursday, June 18, Dasch took a train to Washington, and when he arrived, he called FBI headquarters. This time, he identified himself as "George Davis." He explained that he was the leader of a group of saboteurs sent from Germany and that he had important information he would give only to Hoover. He called again the following morning, and this time, he gave his location: a hotel in Washington. Soon after the call, FBI agents arrived at the hotel, and Dasch was taken into custody and subject to a long interrogation, after which he gave the FBI the names and locations of the other three members in his group. Burger, Quirin, and Henck were all arrested in New York City on June 20 and 21.

Dasch also told the FBI about Kerling's group, something about which they knew nothing. Dasch was not sure when, precisely, the group had landed or where they would initially go. His handkerchief with the invisible writing on it was analyzed by FBI scientists, who discovered the name and addresses of contacts in the country whom *Abwehr* considered reliable. One of these people was Helmut Leiner, a US citizen who emigrated from Germany in the 1930s and now lived on Long Island. His home was watched by FBI agents, and on Tuesday, June 23rd, he was followed when he took the train into New York City. Agents watched as he met with Kerling and one other member of the group, Werner Thiel. Kerling was arrested later the same day and Thiel was arrested on Thursday, June 25th.

That left just two members of the group at large: Herbert Haupt and Hermann Neubauer. Neither the FBI nor their fellow saboteurs had any idea where they were, and the FBI circulated their names and descriptions to all field offices and began a massive manhunt for them. Fortunately, they did not have to look for long. It rapidly became clear that Herbert Haupt had called the FBI office in Chicago on the morning of June 22, apparently wanting to reinforce his cover story, and he told the agent he spoke to a long, rambling story about how he had spent the years when he was not in America and living and working in Mexico. This effort was somewhat wasted as Haupt's name had already been circulated following Dasch's interrogation. Haupt was allowed to leave the FBI office, but he was followed with the hope he would lead the FBI to Hermann Neubauer. He did not, and Haupt was arrested on June 27th. He gave up Neubauer's location under interrogation, and the last saboteur was arrested later the same day.

As a result, less than two weeks after arriving in America, all Pastorius group members were in custody, and none had carried out a single act of sabotage.

The Trial

Following Neubauer's arrest, the FBI released information to the press about the German sabotage teams for the first time. They announced that they had, once again, smashed a potential German spy and sabotage ring, though it failed to mention John Cullen's involvement, that of the Coast Guard, or that Dasch had provided a voluntary confession leading to the conspirators' arrest. Instead, it implied that the FBI's dogged work had identified the spies and led to their arrest alone. When the FBI finally released a detailed report on the events of Operation Pastorius some months later, it still played down the importance of the Coast Guard and made no mention of Dasch's confession.

Soon after the final arrest, all eight men were charged with espionage against the United States. This came as a particularly unpleasant surprise to George Dasch, who clearly thought his surrender and confession should have led to plaudits and not a charge of "Violation of the Laws of War," which carried the death penalty in wartime America.

With the agreement of President Roosevelt, it was decided the men would be tried not in a civilian court, but by a military commission. The president, it seemed, was concerned that action in a civil court would take too long and might not lead to the death penalty. A military court-martial, on the other hand, could be quickly convened, held in secret, and was virtually guaranteed to pass the death sentence if the men were found guilty. Needless to say, with Dasch's confession and the discovery of buried explosives on beaches in Long Island and Florida, this seemed like a foregone conclusion. On June 25, President Roosevelt issued Presidential Proclamation 2561, which read, "All enemies who have entered upon the territory of the United States as part of an invasion or predatory incursion, or who have entered in order to commit sabotage, espionage, or other hostile or warlike acts should be promptly tried in accordance with the laws of war."

The commission that would try the eight men was assembled under Major General Frank R. McCoy, a former commander of the First United States Army's leadership. McCoy was assisted by a panel of six senior officers: three major generals, and three brigadier generals. The prosecution team was headed by Attorney General Francis Biddle and assisted by the US Army's Judge Advocate, General Major General Myron Cramer. The defense consisted of two colonels, Cassius Dowell and Kenneth Royall, with a third colonel, Carl Ristine, appointed as counsel for George Dasch, as Dasch's testimony was certain to be heard by the commission.

McCoy

Biddle

President Roosevelt's request for promptness was heeded. Less than two weeks after the final arrest, on Wednesday, July 8, the military commission began the trial of the eight accused in a conference room in the District of Columbia prison.

The task facing the defense team was formidable. They argued the Pastorius team had carried out no acts of sabotage and that, in fact, the members of the team had never intended to carry out such acts. They also argued that holding the trial under a military commission was illegal as it denied the prisoners a fair hearing and that, since neither Long Island nor Florida were "zones of military operations," it was wrong to try the prisoners before a military commission. None of these arguments were accepted by either the commission or the Supreme Court, to which the defense team eventually appealed. It was clear that the military (and the president) wanted a quick verdict that would deter any potential future acts of espionage against the United States. George Dasch later claimed that even his confession was misrepresented during the trial, portrayed as a cowardly attempt to save himself after his arrest by the FBI and making no mention of his voluntary surrender.

A picture of the trial in July 1942

The Military Commission ended after less than one month on August 3, 1942, and all eight men were found guilty. Kerling, Haupt, Thiel, Henck, Neubauer, and Quirin were sentenced to death, and they were executed five days later in the electric chair at the Washington, D.C. District prison. Dasch was sentenced to 30 years in prison, while Burger, who had also acted as a witness for the prosecution, was given a life sentence.

After the executions, there were more trials of those accused of assisting the Pastorius team. Herbert Haupt's parents, aunt, and uncle, who lived in Chicago, were tried for treason, as were the parents of Wolfgang Wergin, a friend of Haupt, who were also accused of aiding the saboteurs. All were found guilty, and the men were sentenced to death and the women to 25 years in prison. On appeal, the verdicts against the women were overturned, and the sentences for the men were reduced to prison sentences.

In New York, several people were tried for aiding and abetting Dasch and his team, and lengthy sentences in prison were imposed, though these were later reduced under appeal.

The Aftermath of Operation Pastorius

Back in Germany, on June 27, Lahousen, head of *Abwehr* Section II, wrote to Canaris, "We have been receiving Reuters reports of American radio transmission announcing the arrest of all participants in Operation Pastorius, some in New York and some in Chicago. The reports give the correct location of the landings in the United States and of the targets for the planned sabotage operations."

It was clear that Operation Pastorius was not just a complete failure, but a very public fiasco. Even worse, from *Abwehr*'s point of view, this was not the only failed operation it sponsored. Operation Weisdorn in 1942 was an attempt to encourage a popular uprising against British rule in South Africa, and also in 1942, Operation Tiger was an attempt to involve independence movements in India and Afghanistan to engage an armed revolt against British rule. Operation Shamyl in 1941/42 was an attempt to persuade the Muslim population of the Caucasus and Central Asia to revolt against Soviet rule. All of these operations were abject failures that produced no positive results.

After the failure of Operation Pastorius, there was only one further attempt to infiltrate German agents into America. Operation Elster began in late November 1944, when two German agents were dropped by submarine on the coast of Maine. Their mission was to gather intelligence about the American war effort, but they accomplished nothing, and within a month of arriving, one of the agents, William Colepaugh, an American-born defector to Germany, handed himself in to the FBI, betraying the mission and the other agent. Both men were imprisoned for lengthy terms.

Combined with previous failures such as the exposure of spy rings in America by Sebold, German confidence in *Abwehr*'s abilities and those of its leader Canaris was, understandably, not high. In fact, even before the U-boats had left France to take members of the Pastorius group to America, Heydrich made his move to use *Abwehr*'s multiple failures to bring the organization under his control and that of the SS. Canaris was summoned to Prague, where Heydrich had been appointed *Reichsprotektor* of the Protectorate of Bohemia and Moravia, and he was told that, henceforth, all *Abwehr* operations would be carried out under the control and supervision of the SS. However, just a week later, on May 27, before the new arrangements could be finalized, Heydrich was assassinated by soldiers from the Czech's army-in-exile who had been trained and equipped by the British Special Operations Executive.

Heydrich's death may have brought a temporary reprieve from a complete takeover by the SS, but the utter failure of Operation Pastorius underlined *Abwehr*'s seeming inability to effectively undertake one of its core missions: the establishment of intelligence networks and sabotage groups in enemy countries. *Abwehr*'s failings were widely recognized both in the German military and beyond, and there were other theories emerging that *Abwehr* was ineffective not because its leader, Canaris, was inept, but because he was a traitor actively working against Hitler and the Nazis.

As it turned out, the rumors were true, because Germany's spy chief was a double agent who had been passing military secrets to the Allies for years. Canaris would go on to claim he had first become disenchanted with the Nazis after the wave of executions and murders following the Night of the Long Knives in 1934, but his first overt act against the regime took place in late August 1939.

Canaris was invited to attend a briefing given by Hitler and his generals, outlining the military's plan for the invasion of Poland. Taking notes was forbidden, but Canaris, out of sight at the back of the room, was able to jot down some brief reminders. When he returned to his hotel in Munich that evening, he sat down and wrote out everything he could remember about the briefing. Upon returning to Berlin, Canaris passed this information to Colonel Hans Oster, a trusted confederate in *Abwehr*, who handed it to the Dutch military attaché in Berlin. From there, it was passed directly to the British and French intelligence services.

Canaris also began deliberately misleading Hitler. When he learned of the planned invasion of Norway in April 1940, Canaris warned Hitler that this was bound to fail because the British naval presence in the area was so strong that it would destroy the invasion fleet. Hitler went ahead anyway, and Canaris' warning proved to be a false alarm. Fortunately, Hitler and the German general staff concluded that *Abwehr* had simply got it wrong, never guessing that Canaris had invented the information with the hope of preventing the invasion altogether.

In October 1940, Canaris was given control of Operation Felix, a plan to compel General Franco to allow German troops to launch an attack on British-held Gibraltar through neutral Spain. First, Canaris wrote a detailed report explaining why the plan could not succeed. Then, he secretly told the Spanish dictator that Hitler could not spare sufficient troops to mount an invasion of Spain if Franco refused to support Operation Felix. Emboldened by this information, Franco refused to help the Nazis, and Spain officially remained neutral.

Franco

In the fall of 1942, an *Abwehr* agent in Britain submitted a report about a planned Anglo-American invasion of North Africa. The report vanished (Canaris later claimed it had never existed), and the Allied landings in Casablanca, Algiers, and Oran in November came as a complete surprise to German military leaders. The repeated intelligence failures in 1941 and 1942 led to a loss of confidence in *Abwehr* and a diminution of its authority, but Heydrich's death meant the SS was not able to take over its responsibilities completely.

In January 1944, Canaris was given a final chance when he was sent to confer with Field Marshal Albert Kesselring, commander of German forces in the Mediterranean. By that time, the Allies had occupied all of North Africa and Sicily, and Kesselring was worried about rumors of a planned Allied amphibious landing on the coast of Italy. On January 21, Canaris reassured Kesselring and his staff that *Abwehr* had no information about any planned landing on the coast of Italy. The following day, an Anglo-American army of 50,000 men landed at Anzio on Italy's west coast in one of the largest amphibious operations of World War II. As a direct result, Canaris was removed as head of *Abwehr* and replaced with a more fervent Nazi, Walter Schellenberg.

Schellenberg

It is now clear that Canaris was working against the Nazi regime throughout World War II, so it is only natural to wonder whether he deliberately undermined Operation Pastorius, but there is little direct evidence of this. George Dasch was released from an American prison in 1948 and later wrote a book about his involvement in Operation Pastorius.[2] In it, he makes no mention of being given instructions by Canaris to undermine the mission. It is, however, notable that Dasch's appointment as leader of the operation was confirmed by Canaris, and that Dasch was certainly not the most enthusiastic Nazi among the final members of the group. In fact, Dasch had fled America in 1938 simply because he needed to escape an increasingly acrimonious and bigamous marriage. Unlike several of the others who had been early members of the Nazi Party and returned to Germany for ideological reasons, Dasch did not seem particularly interested in supporting the Nazi regime.

It is possible that Canaris recognized this and chose him to head the operation, hoping he would not go through with it. Dasch always claimed that he was an anti-Nazi, and he had never really intended to undertake sabotage in the United States. Whether this is true or (as was claimed at his trial before the military commission) he realized that the mission was doomed when the group was intercepted on the beach at Long Island by John Cullen and tried to save himself will never be known for certain. But what is clear is that Admiral Canaris most certainly was an anti-Nazi who did his best to undermine German military and intelligence operations and regularly passed vital information to the Allies. On several visits to neutral Spain, ostensibly to meet with General Franco on Hitler's behalf, he is thought to have met with British agents from Gibraltar. He also had a long-term relationship with Halina Szymańska, a Polish spy in Switzerland, with whom he regularly met. Through Szymańska, he passed information about major German military plans, including Operation Barbarossa, the plan for the invasion of Russia.

Even after his forced retirement as the leader of *Abwehr* in early 1944, Canaris continued using his contacts to pass information to the Allies. Ahead of the Normandy landings in June 1944, Canaris was somehow able to send the Allies details of the German order-of-battle. All the while, incredibly, he was never suspected by the Germans of passing information to the Allies. All of *Abwehr*'s operational failures occurring under his control were ascribed to incompetence, and there was never any suspicion that he was passing on military intelligence.

Canaris' final downfall and death came about from a quite different set of activities in which he was involved. Like other totalitarian regimes, the leader of the Nazis kept an iron grip on power in part by making sure nobody else could attain too much of it, but as the war progressed and Germany's fortunes faltered, more individuals and groups plotted the death of Hitler.

The climax of these efforts took place on July 20, 1944, but Hitler himself recognized his eminence and notoriety as factors making him the target of assassination attempts years earlier.

---

[2] Dasch 1959

Though his own stated figure of seven attempts to kill him falls on the low end of the actual number of quietly thwarted plots, the Fuhrer knew he was a target and deliberately acted in an elusive fashion. As he stated in 1939, "There will never be anyone in the future with as much authority as I have. My continued existence is therefore a major factor of value. I can, however, be removed at any time by some criminal or idiot. […] no one is safe against some idealist of an assassin who ruthlessly stakes his life for his purpose."

Most assassination schemes against the German dictator centered on the use of bombs to kill him. Such attacks, of course, theoretically increased the chances of killing Hitler, since a blast would create a far larger "fatal area" than a bullet or even a spray of bullets from a submachine gun. Additionally, the bomb's user need not directly risk their own lives or figure out a way to get through Hitler's security, which necessarily watched most closely for human threats rather than completely hidden objects. A few would-be assassins planned a more direct approach, prepared to sacrifice their lives shooting the Fuhrer point blank. Siegfried Knappe, a Wehrmacht major attached to Hitler's bunker staff in the final days in Berlin, expected (incorrectly) that the Russians would execute him and therefore nearly decided to shoot Hitler down with his service pistol. Only the thought that his action would birth a new "Stab in the Back" legend restrained him.

Through it all, Hitler eluded many of the attempts on his life without ever realizing his risk. Most plotters escaped undetected, baffled by the randomness and secretive nature of Hitler's movements. The Fuhrer frequently canceled prearranged engagements, arrived at other locations with only a few minutes' advance notice, used different trains than originally planned, and generally proved constantly unpredictable. When Hitler traveled by air, he not only brought a detachment of fanatical SS guards, but also highly trusted personal physicians and cooks, and his own personal car, the latter armored and already thoroughly checked for sabotage and booby traps.

Beyond all his precautions, the Fuhrer sometimes almost appeared protected by incredible – or uncanny – luck. Despite the enmity of the world and the increasingly violent opposition of his own officers, the Third Reich's leader lived until he chose to die, as though destined by some dark fate to perish only by his own hand.

Even as far back as the late 1930s, Canaris had gathered a group of conspirators who were sworn to remove Hitler and overthrow the Nazi regime. This group, which became known as the *Schwarze Kapelle* ("Black Orchestra"), included members of *Abwehr* and the Wehrmacht, and as early as 1938, some of them had drawn up plans to replace the Nazis with a provisional government. Hitler's political and military successes from 1938 through late 1941 undermined support for the movement, but members of the group continued to pass information to the Allies throughout the war. President Roosevelt's announcement in 1943 that the Allies would not negotiate peace with Germany but would only accept unconditional surrender caused a further loss of support.

Hitler's paranoid mind saw foreign schemers behind every effort to assassinate him. Part of this stemmed from his overwhelming vanity, which made it hard for him to believe a true German could wish to kill such an invaluable asset as himself unless corrupted by foreign agents backed by shadowy Jewish financiers. Additionally, the dictator's contradictory philosophical beliefs played a part. Paradoxically, Hitler declared no force equal to the human "will," but at the same time he refused to believe an individual was capable of acting without a structure of authority to provide them with guidance and inspiration.

Ironically, before the start of the war, British Prime Minister Neville Chamberlain threw away a direct offer from the German high command to depose and probably kill Hitler, which may have averted World War II. In doing so, the British – Hitler's longtime bogeyman and the people he enjoyed blaming for each and every scheme to kill him – may have saved the dictator from overthrow by Oster and his allies by refusing to give even verbal support to their scheme. Chamberlain believed that if he sacrificed enough small states to Hitler's ambition, the Fuhrer would soon grow satisfied and cease his aggression. The British prime minister failed to realize that the German dictator took each new surrender as a sign of trembling pusillanimity and weakness on the part of the British, and that the appeasement policy simply honed and encouraged his boundless schemes of conquest.

Oster had sent a succession of emissaries to Chamberlain and his cabinet throughout the summer of 1938, but as before, the British ignored their pleas with a certain amount of stuffy indignation that the German officers would seek to involve them in something so "underhanded." The English upper class held a deep, essentially racist, loathing for the Germans as well, describing them as "a race of carnivorous sheep."

Finally, on September 5, 1938, Oster and Witzleben led the others in planning a direct coup. They would mobilize Wehrmacht units to neutralize Hitler's SS Liebstandarte bodyguards, seize Hitler, and either kill him immediately or put him on trial for crimes against humanity, almost certainly resulting in a death sentence.

On September 28th, however, Neville Chamberlain destroyed the incipient overthrow of Hitler without even realizing it when the negotiations at Munich led to a peace agreement which effectively granted the Sudetenland to Germany and dismantled his alleged ally Czechoslovakia with the stroke of a pen. This immediately ended any chance of ousting and executing Hitler because the Army commanders prepared to bring their troops to assist the coup only participated due to their fear of war. Now it appeared the Third Reich and Britain would not fight after all, so the Army leaders withdrew their support.

With no soldiers at their command, Oster, Canaris, Witzleben, and the other conspirators could not overcome Hitler's Liebstandarte and seize the Fuhrer. Chamberlain had undone the plot at the eleventh hour by supinely accepting Hitler's demands, and Witzleben, speaking with his fellow conspirators, gave vent to unbridled, savage sarcasm at the disastrous turn of events: "You see, gentlemen, for this poor foolish nation, he is once again our big dearly beloved fuhrer, unique, sent from God, and we, we are a little pile of reactionary and disgruntled officers or politicians who dared to put pebbles in the way of the greatest statesman of all times at the moment of his greatest triumph." (Parssinen, 2003, 166).

Undeterred, Oster continued attempts to overthrow Hitler during the following years. Other officers joined in, but Hitler's elusiveness thwarted several attempts to kill him outright. At one point, Tresckow and a group of other generals prepared to assassinate the Fuhrer during one of his visits to the Russian front by simply pulling out their pistols and riddling him with bullets when he walked into the scheduled briefing. The Fuhrer foiled them by changing his plans and visiting a different part of the front instead.

Another attempt involved a lone suicide bomber – a brave officer who agreed to wear a uniform with a bomb installed in the front of the tunic. When Hitler arrived, the man planned to fling his arms around the Fuhrer and detonate the bomb, killing both Hitler and himself. Several generals invited Hitler to view the "new uniform" they had devised, and the Third Reich's dictator agreed, only to cancel the viewing at the last moment.

The occasion when Tresckow, Oster, and the other military conspirators came closest to killing Hitler took place on March 13th, 1943. Dubbed Operation Flash, the plan involved smuggling a plastic explosive package disguised as a bottle of Cointreau triple sec cognac liqueur aboard Hitler's personal Focke-Wulf Condor aircraft at Smolensk. The sophisticated explosive, timed to detonate with the Condor near Minsk, would tear even the heavily armored aircraft apart. One of the conspirators, Fabian von Schlabrendorff (destined to survive the war, raise six children, work as a constitutional judge in West Germany, and die in 1980 at the age of 73), gave the bottle to Colonel Heinz Brandt at Smolensk, asking him to take the liquor back to headquarters and give it to Colonel Stieff, a personal friend. Schlabrendorff claimed the Cointreau settled a bet with Stieff which he had lost, and Brandt readily agreed to take the cognac with him on the flight.

The conspirators awaited news of the destruction of Hitler's aircraft, but instead learned the Condor landed intact, against all odds, at Rastenburg. Schlabrendorff boldly telephoned Brandt and told him he had given him the wrong bottle. He asked the Colonel to hold it for him overnight, when he would arrive personally at headquarters, retrieve the bottle, and give Stieff the correct bottle personally. Schlabrendorff arrived at headquarters as scheduled and found Colonel Brandt, in an excellent mood, emerging from his office while unwittingly juggling the bomb playfully. Though understandably terrified, Schlabrendorff thanked Brandt, took the bottle, and retreated to a private location to determine why the bomb failed.

Count Claus Schenk von Stauffenberg played the central role in Operation Valkyrie, also known as the July 20th bomb plot, the 1944 attempt on Hitler's life that (unlike most of the Army's previous efforts) nearly succeeded. The subject of numerous books and at least one high-profile popular film, Operation Valkyrie came even closer than Georg Elser's bombing attempt to killing Hitler.

Since at least 1943, Stauffenberg had involved himself in covert resistance to Hitler and scheming against the Fuhrer's life. The officers engaged in these ambitious plans worked out a strategy, "Valkyrie," that would enable the seizure of key spots and the arrest or elimination of crucial Nazi personnel in the event Hitler died, allowing the schemers to assume the reins of power or at least attempt to do so.

Stauffenberg received a promotion to the rank of colonel on July 1st, 1944 and found himself participating in meetings at the Berghof as an aide to General Friedrich Fromm. The newly minted colonel answered summons to appear at the Berghof on July 8th, when Fromm consulted with Hitler and other top officers on the conduct of the war. Stauffenberg smuggled a bomb into the conference room but did not detonate it, perhaps due to the absence of Himmler and Goering, whom the resistance consistently earmarked for elimination at the same time as Hitler to increase the chances of Nazi collapse.

Fromm

The plotters now felt extreme urgency in bringing about Hitler's death, and two factors impelled them: fear of Gestapo discovery, and the Allies' advance. The men hoped to gain a negotiated peace with the Allies rather than an unconditional surrender following their slaying of the Fuhrer, but such an outcome remained possible only as long as the Allies remained outside Germany's borders. Hitler must die before the Allies reached German soil or the plan would be in vain.

The inner circle of men at the heart of the plot – Oster, Stauffenberg and his brother, Canaris, Beck, Tresckow, Schlabrendorff, Witzleben, and other longtime resisters, along with new faces such as Hans-Ulrich von Oertzen, remained conflicted about the plan but determined to proceed despite their personal shame at "betraying" German military obedience. Stauffenberg explained his thoughts several days before the July 20th bombing attempt. While his brother, Berthold von Stauffenberg, judged the attempt foredoomed but declared the necessity of trying in any case. Claus von Stauffenberg remarked, "It is now time that something was done. But he who has the courage to do something must do so in the knowledge that he will go down in German history as a traitor. If he does not do it, however, he will be a traitor to his conscience." (Hoffmann, 1996, 374).

Stauffenberg sought another opportunity to blow up Hitler on July 11th, again at the Berghof. Though he successfully smuggled a bomb into the conference room, Stieff – now in on the plan – dissuaded him from throwing it due to Himmler's absence. It's also possible his courage failed him or he could not bear the stain on his military honor.

On July 14th, Hitler moved his headquarters from the Berghof to the Wolfsschanze ("Wolf's Lair") in Prussia, a massive forest complex near Rastenburg. Stauffenberg accompanied the staff, still carrying his briefcase bomb, and on July 15th, he placed the briefcase in the Wolfsschanze's conference room and left. Before the bomb exploded, however, Stieff entered the room, removed the briefcase, and disarmed the timing mechanism, once again possibly saving Hitler's life.

Bundesarchiv, Bild 101III-Reprich-012-08
Foto: Reprich | 1942

Pictures taken at the Wolf's Lair

Stauffenberg (standing on the far left) next to Hitler on July 15, 1944

On July 19th, dozens of officers prepared for the seizure of key points in Berlin and elsewhere on the following day, along with the broadcast of messages announcing Hitler's death and the end of the Third Reich. Few expected success, least of all Stauffenberg, but all stood ready to carry out their part in the unfolding drama.

Stauffenberg arrived at Rastenburg airport at 10:00 a.m. on July 20th carrying an innocuous briefcase. Meeting fellow conspirator Werner von Haeften shortly before the 12:30 p.m. military conference with Hitler, he gave Haeften the empty briefcase and received the explosive briefcase, containing two bombs, in its place. Stauffenberg armed the first bomb but then found himself interrupted by an urgent telephone call. Apparently slightly panicked, he left the second bomb behind, halving the explosive power of the briefcase and, most likely, accidentally saving

Hitler's life.

When the meeting in the Wolfsschanze's map room with its gigantic oak table finally got underway, Stauffenberg entered and put the explosive briefcase down just three feet from where Hitler stood, behind one of the oak table's massive legs. He then left again, blending in with the aides who hurried in and out, fetching papers, making telephone calls, sending telegraph messages, and the like. At 12:42 p.m., the bomb exploded, as one of the 40 men present later recalled: "In a flash the map room became a scene of stampede and destruction… there was nothing but wounded men groaning, the acrid smell of burning and charred fragments of maps and papers fluttering in the wind." (Moorhouse, 2006, 190).

Many of those present died, and most of the rest suffered wounds, but thanks to the protection offered by the table leg and the table itself, Hitler survived with minor injuries except for perforations in his eardrums. The blast had blown his pants right off of him.

A picture of the damage done by the bomb

For a few hours, things appeared to go the conspirators' way. The Valkyrie troops mobilized and seized a number of key objectives by 6:00 p.m. However, at around this time, Hitler began calling officers he knew, enabling them to recognize his voice and realize he was still alive, and many of the officers soon began standing their troops down. Even Witzleben called off his soldiers and went home by 9:00 p.m. Hitler seemed euphoric at his survival, laughing and joking with the other people at the Wolfsschanze and declaring loudly, over and over again, "I am invulnerable, I am immortal!"

A wave of arrests followed in Germany and France as Gestapo interrogations, captured documents, and the actions of conspirators revealed those who participated in the scheme. Some of the men involved successfully committed suicide before their capture. Tresckow, a longtime plotter against the Fuhrer's life, managed to kill himself on the Eastern Front before the Gestapo or SS arrested him, and indeed before they even suspected him. He arranged to drive out alone with a submachine gun, which he fired, then detonated a grenade against his body to simulate his killing by partisans. Another plotter, Hans-Ulrich von Oertzen, asked to urinate while being arrested. The Gestapo allowed him to use the bathroom in his office, where he thrust a live grenade into his mouth and blew his own head off.

Many, however, fell alive into Gestapo hands and suffered extensive torture as the secret police worked to extract more names and more details from their captives. Beatings, electric shocks, the medieval rack, and a special finger-piercing device were all used during the interrogations. Some displayed their injuries in court, causing consternation in a society not entirely accustomed to the excesses of a dictatorial regime even after 11 years of rule by Adolf Hitler.

Eventually, the People's Court, headed by the notorious, intelligent, and corrupt Roland Freisler, tried dozens of prisoners and condemned them to death. 7,000 arrests led to no less than 4,980 executions, including some which amounted to no more than personal revenge by SS personnel against people they hated.

Ironically, an act of kindness on Oster's part had already led to his undoing. He assisted 14 Jews in obtaining false *Abwehr* identification papers, enabling their escape to Switzerland, but unfortunately the Gestapo arrested his assistant, Hans von Dohnanyi, who funded the escape, on charges of financial corruption. Linked to Dohnanyi, Oster found himself under house arrest, and when his links to several of the July 20th, 1944 plotters emerged, the Gestapo transferred him to a concentration camp, along with Canaris.

Even at this stage, Oster's role in the earlier attempts to overthrow Hitler remained secret until the last days of the war. The Gestapo finally discovered incriminating diaries in early 1945 that detailed *Abwehr's* determination to remove Hitler from power by force and either kill him or declare him criminally insane. The Fuhrer responded with wrath, ordering Oster and all other conspirators executed forthwith. After a brief trial with a foregone conclusion on April 9, 1945, Oster and several other men suffered execution by hanging at Flossenburg concentration camp. Wilhelm Canaris died beside him. Two weeks later, on April 23, 1945, elements of the U.S. 90th Infantry Division liberated the camp, too late to save two of its most notable prisoners.

George Dasch and Ernest Burger were both released from prison in America and deported to Germany in 1948. Neither were welcomed there, as both were regarded as traitors who had betrayed their comrades. Ernest Burger died in Germany in 1975 at the age of 69. George Dasch died in Ludwigshafen, Germany in 1992 at the age of 89.

What is particularly notable about Operation Pastorius and other German espionage missions was just how amateurish they were, especially compared to similar missions undertaken by German agents during World War I. This may, in part, be ascribed to Canaris' desire to see the missions fail, but it also illustrates a fundamental lack of ability in covert operations. It must also be noted that the FBI's response was just as ineffective. Though it was suppressed at the time, historians now know that all of the seeming successes of the FBI against these operations and were due either to the people involved voluntarily surrendering and confessing or to the presence of double agents. At the time, Hoover made sure the American public believed the successes were entirely due to a dogged investigation by FBI agents.

Naturally, the best fiction stories about espionage and counterintelligence tend to depict spies and those who pursue them as clever, cunning, and ruthless, but as Operation Pastorius made clear, the reality is often quite different.

Online Resources

Other World War II titles by Charles River Editors

Other titles about Operation Pastorius on Amazon

Further Reading

Dobbs, Michael, Saboteurs: The Nazi Raid on America, New York: Knopf, 2004. ISBN 0-375-41470-3

Rachlis, Eugene, They Came to Kill: The Story of Eight Nazi Saboteurs in America, New York: Random House, 1961.

Persico, Joseph E., Roosevelt's Secret War: FDR and World War II Espionage, New York:Random House, 2001, pp. 199–205. ISBN 0-375-50246-7

Lippmann, David H., World War II Plus 55, June 10-13th, 1942

Montauk Life: The Night of the Nazis

Cornell University School of Law: Ex Parte Quirin (summary)

Samaha, Joel, et al. (eds.), Transcript of Proceedings before the Military Commission to Try Persons Charged with Offenses against the Law of War and the Articles of War, Washington D.C., 8 to 31 July 1942, Minneapolis: University of Minnesota, 2004. [1]

Abella, Alex & Gordon, Scott, Shadow Enemies: Hitler's Secret Terrorist Plot Against the United States, Guilford, CT: Lyons Press, 2002. ISBN 1-58574-722-X

Free Books by Charles River Editors

We have brand new titles available for free most days of the week. To see which of our titles are currently free, click on this link.

Discounted Books by Charles River Editors

We have titles at a discount price of just 99 cents everyday. To see which of our titles are currently 99 cents, click on this link.